I0158134

Isaac

James Poole

ISBN: 978-1-78364-457-5

The Open Bible Trust
Fordland Mount, Upper Basildon,
Reading, RG8 8LU, UK.

www.obt.org.uk

Isaac

Contents

Page

Introduction

The history of Abraham is vivid with dramatic incident. His response to God's call; going out "not knowing whither he went", from his country and family; to a land that the Lord would show him (Hebrews 11:8; Genesis 12:1); his rescue of his nephew Lot and all his goods from the confederacy of the five kings who had conquered Sodom and Gomorrah (Genesis 14:8-16); to his offering up of Isaac his beloved son, the child of promise, in response to God's command (Genesis 22:1-2; Hebrews 11:17-19). These are just a few instances of many outstanding events in the life of that great man of faith, Abraham.

By contrast the life of Isaac is comparatively quiet and uneventful, no such dramatic incidents occur in the same intensity as in his father's life. Isaac appears to me a sensitive man who felt things keenly. He greatly mourned the death of his mother, Sarah, and was comforted by the advent of Rebekah in his life (Genesis 24:63-67). He seems to have preferred a quiet life, avoiding all strife. In this lay the danger of compromise, and we shall see how the Lord disrupted the calm of his life, in order to teach him to trust Him completely in all things.

Early days

On reading Genesis 22, we tend to be occupied entirely with the supreme act of faith of Abraham. His immediate response to God's command to offer up his young son Isaac as a burnt offering upon one of the mountains that God would show him (Genesis 22:2). Whatever Abraham's feelings were of anxiety and his love for his only son, he said,

> "The Lord will provide a lamb" (Genesis 22:8).

However, it is doubtful if Abraham believed this. Rather he knew that God's promised seed of a great nation, Israel, depended upon Isaac and so to fulfil that promise he

> "accounted that God was able to raise him up from the dead; from whence also he received him in a figure" (Hebrews 11:19).

But what about Isaac? He meekly submitted to his father's will and went with him to the altar. Whatever went through his mind, he trusted his father, Abraham, absolutely.

Is not Isaac a perfect type of our Lord Jesus Christ Who went to Calvary's cross willingly in obedience to His Father's will? Unlike the ram caught in a thicket, which was an unwilling sacrifice, Christ was the willing Lamb of God in His sacrifice for us. Yet those words of Abraham, "The Lord will provide a lamb", whether spoken in belief of unbelief, turned out to be prophetic!

The choice of Isaac's wife, Rebekah (Genesis 24:1-67)

Abraham's godly fear lest his son Isaac should be married to a Canaanite woman, caused him to make careful preparation to ensure that a wife was sought from his country and relatives. This indicated great concern that the line of his seed would not be contaminated. Thus he made his eldest servant (possibly Eliezer of Damascus - Genesis 15:2-4) swear on oath not to take a wife for Isaac from the Canaanites.

Abraham's servant, zealous to carry out his task faithfully, committed the whole matter to the Lord God for guidance (c.f. Proverbs 3:5-6) and departed with ten camels to Mesopotamia to the city of Nahor. He arrived in the evening, the time that the women went out to draw water. Pondering the next step to take, he asked the Lord to accept a sign that on his request for water, a young woman would not only give drink to him, but also yo his camels. This would be an unusual kindness on her part, but an answer to his prayers that she should be the wife for Isaac.

Before he had done praying, a young woman, Rebekah, came to draw water. She was a beautiful virgin and fulfilled the sign that the servant had prayed for. She not only gave water to him on request, but also offered to water his camels. To make doubly sure, he asked Rebekah whose daughter she was and if there was room enough in her father's house to lodge both him and his camels. She replied that she was the daughter of Bethuel, the son of Milcah, whose husband was Nahor and that there was room to lodge him and his camels. Upon hearing this, the servant of Abraham bowed his head and worshipped the Lord with profound thanks for answered prayer.

Surely Abraham's servant is a model for all of us in all our problems.

> "In all thy ways acknowledge Him and he shall direct (rightly divide) thy paths" (Proverbs 3:5,6).

Laban and his household gave generous hospitality to Abraham's servant, feasting him well and providing accommodation for him and his camels for the night. Such lavish hospitality doubtless came from ulterior motives.

Laban, Rebekah's brother, as we know, was a covetous man. The way he treated Jacob later on was typical of his meanness. He extracted as much labour from Jacob as he could for a meagre return for his service.

He promised Rachel his daughter to be Jacob's wife after seven years service. However, he then went back on his word by substituting Leah, his other daughter, instead, and Jacob had to work a further seven years for Rachel. It is significant that on seeing his sister, Rebekah, his covetous eyes noted the nose ring and the bracelets on his sister's wrists (Genesis 24:30). No doubt he saw a prospect of enrichment for himself.

After Abraham's servant had recounted his mission from home, and the way the Lord had led him, Laban and Bethuel agreed to let Rachel go to be Isaac's wife. However, there was an attempted delay.

They requested that Rebekah be allowed to stay for at least ten days with them, before departing. Was this an attempt to gain enrichment? Or perhaps they hoped Rebekah may have second thoughts. Or it may have been an attempt by Satan to delay the bride for the promised seed.

Whatever the reason, Abraham's servant was adamant to leave without delay, in spite of a further attempt to delay Rebekah's departure, by asking her if she was willing to go. Unhesitatingly she said "I will go" (v 58). The Lord had called her, and like Lydia, Rebekah offered her heart to obey Him (Acts 16:14).

While Rebekah was journeying to meet Isaac, we read that he "went out to meditate in the fields in the evening" (v 63). E W Bullinger has a note in *The Companion Bible* on "meditate". This refers back to the historical context (Genesis 23:19), to the death and burial of Sarah, Isaac's mother. What follows this digression (of which Isaac as yet knew nothing), in chapter 24:1-67, shows that Isaac went out not to "meditate", or to pray (*KJV* margin), or take a walk (*Syriac*) or muster the flocks (*Gesenius*) but "to mourn". This is the meaning of the Hebrew *shuach* in Psalm 44:25 and Lamentations 3:20. This surely is correct, for Isaac was comforted by Rebekah, after his mother's death.

Isaac the man

Isaac's life was in two phases.

(1) 26:1   The Famine
     26:2-5   The Lord's first appearance to
                 him
     26:6-22   Lack of faith in the Lord

(2) 26:23   The Journey to Beersheba
     26:24   The Lord's second appearance to
                 him
     26:25-33   Trust in the Lord.

"And it came to pass after the death of Abraham, that God blessed Isaac his son, and Isaac dwelt by the well Lahai-roi ... and there was a famine in the land beside the first famine that was in the days of Abraham" (Genesis 25:11 and 26:1).

The blessing of Isaac by God was followed by a famine in the land. Our adversary, Satan, is ever on the alert to oppose the blessings which God graciously gives and to hinder at every stage the road to spiritual progress.

Just like it was in the case of Abraham, the blessing received by Isaac was contested by Satan to intimidate Isaac in his witness for God, to weaken his resolve.

Satan's tactics never vary, in fact they are repeated again and again. He begins by attacking our trust in God and we lose the consciousness of His presence. Material and sensual things are substituted for spiritual desires and we become completely occupied with self.

The first appearance of God to Isaac

Famine undermined Isaac. He lost confidence in the future. Fear took its place as he journeyed to Abimelech, king of the Philistines, to Gerar. It looked as if Isaac intended to journey to Egypt and so God appeared unto Isaac to foil the project and said:

> "Go not down to Egypt; dwell in the land which I shall tell thee of: sojourn in this land and I will be with thee and bless thee; for unto thee and unto thy seed, I will give all those countries, and I will perform the oath which I swore unto Abraham thy father; and I will make thy seed to multiply as the stars of heaven and will give unto thy seed all these countries; and in thy seed shall all the nations of the earth be blessed; because that Abraham obeyed my voice and kept my charge, my commandments, my statutes and my laws." (Genesis 26:2-5)

The Lord who leads His people, supplies their needs, provides food for His children in due season and teaches each lesson at precisely the right time. His gracious promise was the very thing needed to encourage Isaac at this junction. The famine had marred the blessing hitherto enjoyed, casting a shadow across Isaac's faith. Going to Philistia had upset his daily routine and fear for the future had taken its place.

The command to

"Dwell in the land"

was given by God to strengthen and stabilize Isaac. Likewise the promise that

"I will be with thee and I will bless thee" (Genesis 26:3).

To Isaac there were dark clouds on the horizon. These words were to him a shield and a guarantee to protect him in the presence of the Philistines and to calm his fears brought about by the famine.

The great lesson here in the school of life is to teach us the insufficiency of self and the all sufficiency of God.

The journey of the people of Israel through the wilderness after leaving Egypt was designed by God to teach this lesson to them. What beats mankind so often is the over-estimation of our own strength and the underestimation of God's power.

> "Whatsoever Jehovah hath spoken we will do" (Exodus 19:8),

signified Israel's self-confidence, but the journey from the Red Sea to Sinai, was a long series of murmurings and rebellions against the way that the Lord led them.

> "Can He provide a table in the wilderness?" (Psalm 78:19).

This question shows their lack of faith in the Lord. The history of Israel is a catalogue of rebellion and departure from Almighty God. How wonderful was the graciousness of the Lord shown in pardoning their transgressions time after time!

When we acknowledge our moral failure and cast ourselves upon the Lord, a greater realisation of Him and His power is experienced. Through adversity He leads us to a new sphere and bids us look upon life from a new angle. Trials are but examinations to reveal to us the grade attained in the school of faith. They encourage us to view the possibilities that lie ahead if we will only renounce confidence in the flesh and trust in the Lord's love alone.

Isaac's faith in God's promises was weak and he leaned upon his own ability to handle the situation he was in. The thoughts and opinions of men can dominate us when our faith in God is weak. The peace-giving promise "I will be with thee" did not overshadow Isaac. The fear of man took over and he sought to placate the "men of the place". He feared to disclose that Rebekah was his wife, "lest the men of the place should kill him". Fear for his life, "lest I die for this", motivated all his actions.

Isaac's lie about his wife Rebekah ("she is my sister"), in process of time was discovered. He gave himself away by his own behaviour to her. Being found out, Isaac confessed to his lie, stating the cause which had promoted it. "Lies are short-legged", is an Italian proverb. What it means is that truth will out in God's good time. Isaac had such a practical demonstration of this truth, that he was not likely to forget it again.

Fear is contagious. Not only was Isaac afraid of the Philistines, but Abimelech became afraid of him. He remembered his experience with Abraham. Although he was innocent, he remembered God's word to him in the visions of the night

> "thou art but a dead man ... if thou restore her not, know thou that thou shalt surely die, thou and all that are thine".

Abraham's son Isaac, following his father's tactics, had brought Abimelech's kingdom face to face with destruction and his country laid open to disaster, just as it had been with Abraham.

Abimelech, fearful of a possible catastrophe, issued a decree. "He that touches the man or his wife, shall surely be put to death."

Isaac now has nothing to fear! His diplomacy, overruled by God, had given him rest. The "men of the place" were restrained from harming him or his wife by the king's decree. The secular arm protected him from interference, so he devotes himself to agriculture, farms a district and sows seed. The Lord blessed him a hundredfold and he progressively became very great. His flocks and herds multiplied and his household became great. How faithfully the Lord remained true to His promise of blessing Isaac, in spite of his unfaithfulness.

"He abides faithful, he cannot deny himself" (2 Timothy 2:13).

The peace that Isaac received was not permanent. The trial was over but it is easy to pass from moral strait and stress to a period which leads to moral lethargy and the approach of spiritual insensibility. Many a time the achievement of a desired end, leads to spiritual stagnation. But the Lord has a wonderful way of startling His servants out of the even tenor of their way.

Deep and wonderful is the principle underlying God's disciplinary methods. He punished His people Israel with the very things for the sake of which they sold His glory. Take the case of Asa, king of Judah. At the start of his reign, he was faced with an attack by Zera, the Ethiopian, who came against him with an army of three thousand, three hundred chariots. Asa prayed to the Lord and said:

> "Lord, there is none beside thee to help, between the mighty and him that hath no strength: help us O Lord, our God; for we rely on Thee and in Thy Name we are come against the multitude." (2 Chronicles 14:11, *RV*)

The Lord answered the King's prayer and delivered him with a great victory over the Ethiopians. The king of Judah had rest for thirty years. Many Israelites of the Northern Kingdom fell to him in abundance when they saw that the Lord his God was with him (2 Chronicles 14:9-15:9).

Towards the close of Asa's reign the King of Israel went up against Judah and built Ramah, to prevent any further exodus of his subjects to Judah. But Asa did not seek the Lord's help as he had done against the Ethiopians. He robbed the treasury of the Temple and sent a present to the King of Syria with a request that he would

> "Go break thy league with Baasha, King of Israel, that he may depart from me" (2 Chronicles 16:3).

The King of Syria harkened to Asa and invaded Samaria, forcing Baasha to withdraw from the territory of Judah, and abandon the building of fortifications. Asa wanted to avoid war. He thought that he had gained his objective and possibly prided himself on the outcome of his negotiations. But God's thoughts are not our thoughts! When Asa returned to Jerusalem, the prophet met him with the following message:

"Were not the Ethiopians and the Lubim a huge host, with chariots and horsemen exceeding many? Yet, because thou didst rely on the Lord, He delivered them into thin hand. For the eyes of the Lord run to and from throughout the whole earth, to show himself strong on behalf of those whose hearts are perfect towards Him. Herein thou hast done foolishly; for from henceforth thou shalt have wars." (2 Chronicles 16:8-9, *RV*)

This was the very thing Asa endeavoured to avert. He sold the interests of God to avoid war, and God punished him with war!

Isaac employed cunning to avoid strife and God punished him with strife! This is a solemn principle to lay to heart! Isaac's great wealth alarmed the Philistines. Here was an alien who could be a menace to them. Their animosity was roused to a high pitch and there was a cry for vengeance. The situation was critical. Abimelech feared that his subjects might take some action against Isaac that would bring God's judgement upon them all. Quarrels arose between the servants of Isaac and the herdsmen of Gerar. King Abimelech was in a dilemma. He, according to his wisdom, ordered Isaac to leave,

> "Go from us for thou art much mightier than we" (Genesis 26:16).

Isaac's great wealth and possessions, which he acquired under the king's protection, had become a menace to the inhabitants of the land. Isaac did not appear eager to move and lingered in the valley of Gerar. There he dug two wells, causing strife between his servants and the local herdsmen. He moved on and dug another well, for which there was no striving. Isaac interprets the absence of strife as the Divine will of God,

> "Now the Lord hath made room for us, and we shall be fruitful in the land" (Genesis 26:22).

On the strength of this intimation, Isaac moved towards Beersheba. A new era was about to dawn for him.

The Philistines

Here it would be a good thing to digress and ask ourselves the question, who were these Philistines who had caused so much trouble to Isaac? What did they stand for and what was their religion? One of the first things we notice is that the Philistines tended towards abnormal development. They were giants, some having twelve fingers and twelve toes. David's servants slew four such giants (2 Samuel 21:15-21).

When David encountered Goliath, the Philistines encamped at Ephes-dammim (1 Samuel 17:1). When Samson was captured by the Philistines, they sacrificed to their god, Dagon. This was the national god of the Philistines, whose most famous temples were at Gaza and Ashdod. Its form had the face and hands of a man, and the tail of a fish. "Call for Samson" (they said) "that he may make us sport" (Judges 16:25). They wanted revenge and amusement with Samson satisfied it.

They exhibited bitter hostility towards Israel. In the days of the Patriarchs, they filled their wells with sand (Genesis 21:25; 26:15).

During the period of the Judges, all the smiths in Israel were removed to prevent the manufacture of arms. Thus

> "in the day of battle there was neither sword nor spear found with any of the people" (1 Samuel 13:22 c.f. also verse 19).

Their aim was to render the people of God resourceless and defenceless by depriving them of water and the sword. Spiritually, water represents life and the sword the means of defence. These are both symbols of the Word of God (Ephesians 5:26; 6:17). The Philistines demolished the shield of faith, which had been for centuries the strength and comfort of the people of God. No substitute was offered for what they took away.

To sum up:
Formalism, amusement, destructiveness, and the cultivation of abnormal tastes were some of the

features of their society (also sexual immorality may have been part of their worship as it was in other pagan religions). Are not these tendencies much in evidence today? Their spirit still lives and opposes the forces of God. In *some* churches, hybrid, bloodless gospels are preached; icy formalism and a crass, destructive criticism, the product of human theology, sap their very life, while excessive fun and frolic rule the hour and sexual morality tends to be compromised. E W Bullinger once said

> "The duty of a Pastor is to feed the sheep, not to amuse the goats!"

In saying this I do not want to give the impression that *moderate* use of recreation and a sanctified sense of humour is to be ignored. Shall we who know the value of the precious blood of Christ and the grace of God's Holy Spirit, be intimidated by the advance of the Philistine horde? Stand fast in the armour of God[1] (Ephesians 6:10-18). The

---

[1] For more on this see *The Armour of God* by James Poole, published by The Open Bible Trust.

Philistine warriors, in spite of their great stature and huge weapons, were no match for David and his servants, who relied on the Lord for victory. Those who withstood them in the name of the Lord found that the Philistines, in spite of their outward show, were nerveless in battle. Let us gird our loins in God's truth and, staunch in heart and devotion, put to flight the enemies of God, who harass the church from within!

The second appearance of the Lord to Isaac

The journey to Beersheba was a step in the right direction. By what is called force of circumstance, Isaac is guided back in the will of the Lord into the divine path. When Isaac reached Beersheba, the Lord appeared unto Isaac the same night and said:

> "I am the God of Abraham thy father: fear not, for I am with thee, and will bless thee and multiply thy seed greatly for my servant Abraham's sake." (Genesis 26:24, *RV*)

"Fear not, for I am with thee." How patient the Lord is with us, time and again repeating the lessons we have failed to learn. Isaac, emboldened by the Lord's words, built an altar, called upon the name of Jehovah, and pitched his tent, showing that he meant to stay (c.f. Abraham, Genesis 12:8). This was an open avowal of his allegiance to the

Lord and dependence upon Him for protection. A well was dug at this place by Isaac's servants.

Abimelech then visited Isaac and noted the digging of a well, indicating Isaac's determination to take a stand. With Abimelech was Ahuzzath his friend and Phichol the captain of his host, but Isaac feared not for he trusted that the Lord was with him. The Philistines now began to watch Isaac closely. They wondered what would become of the man, whose welfare, they thought, depended on their favour. They were amazed to see his prosperity increasing, the blessing of Isaac doubles and he waxes very great. No one could stand before him.

Abimelech is now convinced, together with Ahuzzath his friend and Phichol the captain of his host, in a consensus of opinion, that Isaac's prosperity depended not on his patronage but on the God, whose name Isaac invoked, and the fear of God fell upon the Philistines. Isaac asked Abimelech why he had come to visit him and Abimelech replied:

"We saw certainly that the Lord was with thee and we said, 'Let there now be an oath betwixt us, even betwixt us and thee and let us make a covenant with thee; that thou wilt do us no hurt, as we have not touched thee and as we have done unto thee nothing but good and have sent thee away in peace:' thou art now the blessed of the Lord." (Genesis 26:28-29)

This was equally true before, no less than after; *but Isaac's conduct had veiled the movements of God's arm and befogged His operations.* But when Isaac publicly relied on Jehovah, the truth blazed in full radiance to his opponents. The working of God is now seen by all and acknowledged. His enemies confess the power of God and seek reconciliation with His servant. Isaac also sees the fulfilment of the Lord's promise to Abraham, under oath on Mount Moriah;

"Thy seed shall possess *the gate* of their enemies" (Genesis 22:17).

Abimelech's visit to Isaac with the company of his friend and captain of his host, was a manifest token of Jehovah's working. Surely the great lesson for us in God's protection and dealing with Isaac is:

> The fear of man bringeth a snare: but whoso putteth his trust in the Lord, shall be safe. (Proverbs 29:5)

The final episode

The blessing of Jacob and Esau lies outside this study, but its personal bearing on Isaac's faith, concludes the record of his life.

Before the final episode of Isaac's life is commented on, a question may be asked. Did Rebekah, after enquiring of the Lord, concerning the struggle in her womb, communicate what He told her to Isaac?

> "Two nations are in thy womb, and two manner of people shall be separated from thy bowels; and the one people shall be stronger than the other people; and the elder shall serve the younger." (Genesis 25:23)

We are not told that Rebekah informed her husband Isaac of the Lord's revelation to her about the elder son serving the younger. It is not recorded in scripture that she did. However, we cannot be certain that Isaac was not told. If Isaac was not told, he would naturally assume that Esau, his elder son would inherit the blessing of the birthright. Furthermore, Rebekah would attempt to ensure that Jacob should receive the blessing. In other words she tried "to help God" (c.f. Uzzah who also tried to help God 2 Samuel 6:6-7).

When the two boys grew up, they manifested widely differing temperaments. Esau, who like his father, was a tiller of the field, endearing himself to Isaac. Jacob, a plain man, helped his mother Rebekah in her domestic duties, and won her favour; for a mother always loves more a son who stays at home.

Now when the time to bestow the blessing of the birthright arrived, the Word of God was bound to overrule the will of Isaac, who thought he was blessing Esau. Isaac was deceived by Rebekah's fraudulent scheme, but not God, and the tide of circumstances went contrary to Rebekah's cherished hopes of having her son with her always. Both Isaac and Rebekah allowed personal considerations to influence their conduct.

With a plain, unmistakable statement of God's will, given to Rebekah, Isaac was deceived into acting in a manner dramatically opposed to it. I may be in error in assuming that Isaac was ignorant of God's will and purpose. I give this as my personal thoughts on the subject. Readers must be sure in their own minds, as to where the truth lies.

Rebekah finds herself on God's side, only because His purpose happens to coincide with her own desires. She is orthodox; yet orthodoxy is not a product of conviction but of taste: she fights not for what is right, but for what she likes: she uses every means at her command to defend her position; not because the cause of truth is bound up with it, but because her wishes are assailed. Is it any wonder then if the means employed in her defence are defective? Controversial methods can be no higher than controversial motives!

Rebekah may have argued herself into believing that in fighting for her ends, she was defending the truth; but in reading her acts at this distance of time, we readily perceive that her clamour was but the resentment of ruffled sensibility. However, it was *Isaac's faith* in God's overruling of his mistaken act of preferring Esau that Hebrews exalts.

> "By faith Isaac blessed Jacob and Esau concerning things to come." (Hebrews 11:20)

In Hebrews 11, the gallery of God's faithful ones, this is the only mention of Isaac's faith. It is his supreme act in overcoming the will of the flesh. It is interesting to compare the *King James Version* with the *New International Version* concerning the blessing given to Isaac.

KJV - "Behold thy dwelling shall be the fatness of the earth and the dew of heaven from above, and by thy sword shalt thou live and shalt serve thy brother; and it shall come to pass when thou shalt have the dominion, that thou shalt break his yoke from off thy neck." (Genesis 27:39-40)

NIV - "Your dwelling will be *away from* earth's richness, *away from* the dew of heaven above. You will live by the sword and you will serve your brother. But when you grow restless, you will throw his yoke from off your neck."

Compare with the *KJV* above. I am inclined to agree with the *NIV*.

God's supreme over-ruling will

It is surely this; God works

> "all things after the counsel of his own will" (Ephesians 1:11).

Nothing can frustrate His plans, either for Israel in the future Kingdom of heaven upon earth, (based on His promise to Abraham and reiterated to Isaac, Jacob and Joseph), or for the body of believers, in this administration of grace,

> "chosen in Christ, before the foundation of the world ... [and] ... blessed with all spiritual blessings in Christ in heavenly places in Christ" (Ephesians 1:3-4).

Each individually chosen saint shall be conformed to the Image of His Son (Romans 8:29-30). Neither Satan nor the flesh can frustrate this! We may lapse in faith and walk, causing ourselves distress, but the Lord will never leave us nor forsake us, and by His chastening as our heavenly Father, He will lead us back to a full trust in Him, as He did with Isaac. Let us

> "trust in the Lord with all thine heart and lean not unto thine own understanding" (Proverbs 3:5,6).

Conclusion

It is our own faith, rooted in Christ's faithfulness, that overcomes the world, the flesh and Satan; not a blind incredulous faith, but faith based upon what God has said in His Word. "It is written", rightly divided, is more than a match for Satan.

> "The grace of God that brings salvation, has appeared to all mankind, teaching us that denying ungodliness and worldly lusts, we should live soberly, righteously and godly in this present world, looking for that blessed hope, even the glorious appearing of the great God and our Saviour Jesus Christ" (Titus 2:11-13).

More on Isaac

Portraits of the Patriarchs

By William Henry, Andrew Marple, Michael Penny and Sylvia Penny

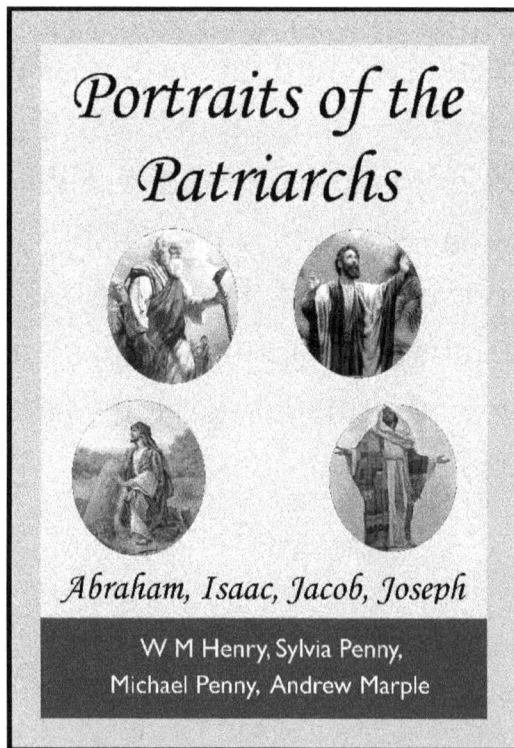

Portraits of the Patriarchs is based on Abraham, Isaac, Jacob and Joseph.

The four authors do an excellent job of not only bringing before us the important issues in the lives of the four patriarchs (i.e. lessons in history). However, they also, in considering the lives and experiences of Abraham, Isaac, Jacob and Joseph, draw out lessons of faith and practice which are applicable to 21st century Christians.

****

Further details of this book can be seen on
www.obt.org.uk

It can be ordered from the website
and also from

The Open Bible Trust,
Fordland Mount, Upper Basildon,
Reading, RG8 8LU, UK.

It also available as an eBook
from Amazon and Apple,
and also as a KDP paperback from Amazon.

Free sample

For a free sample of
the Open Bible Trust's magazine *Search*,
please email

admin@obt.org.uk

or visit

www.obt.org.uk/search

About the author

James Poole was born in Finchley, London, in 1909 and took a course in Business Training at the City of London College. During his working years he was employed by various institutions and banks in the City of London. When he wrote this booklet he was enjoying retirement with his wife in Eastbourne, Sussex, but has since fallen asleep in Christ.

Also by James Poole

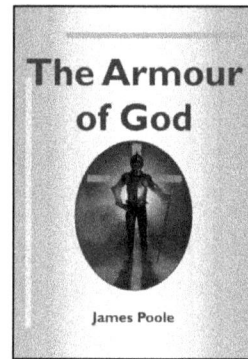

Abraham

James Poole

Isaac

James Poole

Jacob

James Poole

Joseph

James Poole

Notes on Ephesians

James Poole

The Armour of God

James Poole

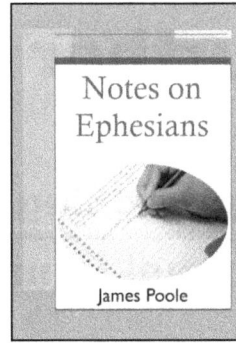

Further details of all the books here can be seen
on **www.obt.org.uk**

The can be ordered from the website
and also from

The Open Bible Trust,
Fordland Mount, Upper Basildon,
Reading, RG8 8LU, UK.

They are also available as eBooks
from Amazon and Apple,
and also as KDP paperbacks from Amazon.

Further Reading

Approaching the Bible
Michael Penny

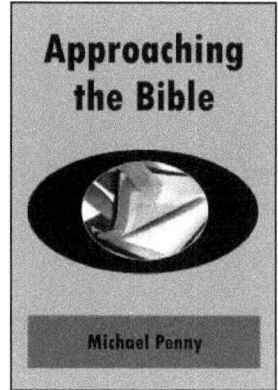

In easy to understand steps, and with many interesting examples, Michael Penny provides the rational for the view that before we try to *apply* any passage in the Bible to ourselves, we should discover first what it meant to those to whom its words were initially addressed. The book advocates that this is best done by considering the passage under the following headings:

1) **W**ho said or wrote it;
2) to **W**hom was it said or written, or concerning **W**hom was it said or written;
3) **W**here it was said or written, or concerning **W**here was it said or written;
4) **W**hat was said or written;

5) **W**hen was it said or written, or concerning **W**hen was it said or written;

6) **W**hy was it said or written.

Applying these six **"W"** rules puts the passage into its proper context and gives us the right perspective on it. Only after doing this can we determine:

7) **W**hether the passage applies to our situation and what the correct application is.

It is the *consistent* use of these **Seven Ws** which helps us discover the right and relevant application of any passage to our lives.

****

This book, and the one on the next page, can be ordered from **www.obt.org.uk** and from

The Open Bible Trust,
Fordland Mount, Upper Basildon,
Reading, RG8 8LU, UK.

40 Problem Passages
Michael Penny

This book is a sequel to *Approaching the Bible*.

The 7 Ws advocated in *Approaching the Bible* are applied to 40 difficult to understand passages. There are, of course, far more than 40 Problem Passages in the Bible. However, in this book Michael Penny not only solves these *40 Problem Passages*, but in doing so he equips the reader with a method by which many, many more hard to understand and difficult passages can be understood and successfully applied to the life of the believer today.

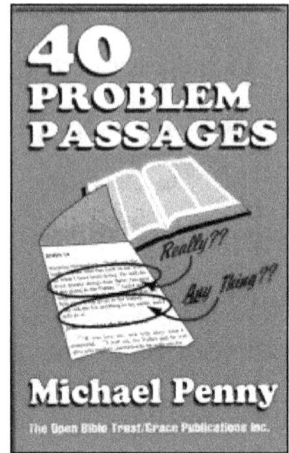

****

This book, and the ones on the previous pages, are also available as eBooks from Amazon and Apple,

and also as KDP paperbacks from Amazon.

About this book

Isaac

The Bible contains many references to Abraham, Isaac and Jacob, and Genesis says so much about the lives of Abraham and Jacob.

By contrast the life of Isaac is comparatively quiet and uneventful, no such dramatic incidents occur in the same intensity as in his father's life or in his son's. If we wonder why he is included with such giants as Abraham and Jacob, then this publication gives us the answer, providing us with important details about Isaac's life and faith.

www.ingramcontent.com/pod-product-compliance
Lightning Source LLC
Chambersburg PA
CBHW060619030426
42337CB00018B/3117